METHOD OF THOUGHT

Frank Karan

Matchstick Literary
1-888-306-8885
orders@matchliterary.com

PREFACE

Frank Karan put forth the idea that we all
need to have a "Method of Thought"
in order to get things done.
Whether it's a sporting club or a government department or a space
Agency, a multinational organization. Or even a
theatre company, a dance troupe rock group
We all need to incorporate a "Method of Thought".

AFFECTIONATE TEAR

Your feet are poised firm against the windowsill
Are you going to jump off or will you stay still
Then I grab you by your freshly painted toenails
Kissing your slender legs with affectionate rear

The anatomy of pain dance freely on my vein
I can't precisely guess what's on you're mind
Especially after you drank so much shiraz wine
Why harbor ill thoughts; docked in small ports

So what's revved u engine without mag wheels
Or a scarry hunting ghost without eerie chills
A large jug of tropical fresh pineapple juice is
Tingling in the sun, titilating fun for everyone

BEAUTY RISES ABOVE THE WEEDS

I leave you love so sweet
To steer a course complete
Hailstones hit hard the ground
Causing tiny puddles to be found

Beauty rises above the weeds
Remaining soft for all to see
Fearing pain is nothing more; than
The brainchild of the desolate poor

Sparkling rhythms of mental health
Help you to see with greater wealth
Reflections of fantasies enter my mind
Clouding clarity for a theatrical time

Obscuring measure for meaningful treasure
Into the foggy twilight I hastily descend
Candle lit low, come near me dear friend
Reconcile your thoughts, for a timid end

BEYOND AND ABOVE

It's called the lonely lover's triangle
When your pounding heart doesn't dangle
All of our senses rotate then mangle
Are we pivoting upon the same angle?

Or spiraling somewhat vainly from diagonal
I'm not seeking any spiritual enlightenment
Or some spontaneous adrenalizing excitement
All I seek is pure, calm nurturing and rest

To deter the ferocious, predating pest
I've been ensnared in this web of zest
Where beauty is revered and worn like a glove
Are your senses ready to go beyond and above?

CATHARTIC SPIKE

I don't want to overcook the pot
Or fill up on your depleted stock
I'm not going to take a bite out of
The cherry, or slice the fruit berry

You're idling on a broken down locomotive
Track yet your itching to blow your stack
How can I be sure when you're totally unsure
And less willing to share whatever you score

What secrets do you hide behind the webbing
Cupboard draw? The afternoon mood is becoming
Trite and lacking sturdy might; it's up to us
To clean out the smelly blocked cathartic spike

CHOKING SMILE

In a juxtaposition of indescribably loathsome
Eau de rie beveraging from stale, empty smoky
Coffee tables' the barstool elusively echoes it's
Unconfined larrikin harmonies metamorphosing into

A pithy grave inscrutable choking smile
There's an unsewered gustative regimen as
I'm bumped n' sloshed in the cynosure of
Unconstructive terminology; pertaining to
A subtle impresario claustrophobically attacking my
Lame spindly windpipe, and uncomposed choking smile
The moonlight glides off the chimney stack as I keep twisting
Through the misty morning haze, longing for the summer's rays

CONTENTIOUSLY RELINQUISHING

You're envisioned virtuous life, has failed to materialize
However revised by the infinite variations of ego coddling
Contentiously relinquishing the devisively blunt burlesque
Into the remissible costumes of everchallenging Romanesque

Like a roughshod headless horse, riding wildly in the night
To reclaim the spotlight; beneficiently rescuing all you're
Boyish frightened friends by outwitting a knavish extremity
Unmistakably protruding into the upper echelons of calamity

CONVENT OF
GOOD SHEPHERD

I remember one mild sunny Saturday afternoon
I was doing extra work; on an upcoming movie
About autistic children; the director's assistant
Yelled out that's a rap, everyone break for lunch

I felt that I wasn't really hungry at all
But I lay captivated by the intricate and
Dazzling architecture of the grand old style
Colonial building, I was wandering around an

I felt like someone out of Alice in the Wonderland
Looking about I saw billy goats grazing in the
Kneehigh grass n' low lying pastures of it's gentle
Rolling hills, peacefully mundane they stood still

The white roses, lilacs and pasted coloured gardenia's
Were immaculately kept n' privoted softly when windswept
Bees were hovering around their hive as I was happily
Swinging to the fragrant jive, an inkling of fandango

In my plucky stride, I then embarked to the second level of
The Convent of Good Shepherd, which has kindly bore host to
Many weary traveller's for the most part of the last century
In one gigantic splendid room there lay a collection of huge

Treasures, hauled in from some flotsam adventures from cargo
  Ship that have vanished without a trace surely now they can
Rest their case; as I made my way upto the pristine belltower
There was lofty hangman's noose, which spellbinded me a bit

  I suddenly gazed at it in awe; trying to figure out what was
    It's explicit purpose, or what role did it mysteriously play
Over the past decades. A soft sunken tiny voice croached out
As I flounced around to see whom it was, I detected a pretty

  Little girl dressed in mozetta white; beaming in a heavenly
  Light, was she an angel or ghost, or some consummate host
    After a brief analytical period of merognostic erotesis and
Acerbating psychological thoughtfulness, and deep inquiring

CONVENT OF GOOD SHEPHERD

I learned that the gardener of the convent was
Deeply in love with a nun but she sworn to
Celibacy so he could not marry her, this drove
Him to so much irritating despair that he went

An wrapped his neck around the hangman's noose
Dangling the ropes in the belltower as he hung
Himself, what a sorry story! I felt as though i
Was trapped n' missed something majestic in time

A winding and wavering bundle of rays from blazing sunlight
Slammed piercingly angry into the belltower where I exhumed
Most of my lunchtime hour, the temptation was bluntly intense
That I too felt the urge to put my neck into the glory noose

When I finally placed the rugged rope around my tender neck
I honestly thought that I'd be hanging on the pirate's deck
Shipwrecked and stranded with only loneliness to sadly shed
I felt the grinding brittle, mangy rope scratching hungrily

Against my virgin skin issuing it's forcible merciless sin
As myself and time stood still I summoned the power within
Legend has it; that whoever puts the trudging dust noose
Around their neck, will in turn suffer the agonizing peck

CORUSCATING THE ATTROCITIES

You're like a savage guillotining ghost ship
Trawling the slivering hungry lubricious sea
Cruising obnoxiously into the empty foggy mist
Capsizing from the brindling, lightning storms

Your slothful mind slithers with it's dull
Gargling slosh, enticed by vernacular cosh
Coruscating the atrocities an animosities
From a timeless period in our human myriad

We're living in between different separate worlds
One is day one is night, one is dark one is light
One is warm one is cold, one is weak one is bold
Will we ever learn, to responsibly take control?

CONVERT DEMEANOR

Courteously chattering in a whistleful tone an
A large peevish stare, you devolve antiquarian
Exhortations denouncing imperfect exclamations
The old idling dogs worry the frightened sheep

So there's chilling flutter beneath my feet
Gently I wipe the perspiration from your pale
Brooding face; and the stressful anticipation
From society's anxious falling grace! Where's

The gentility in you're ill advised covert demeanour
Elastically we clutter amongst the angst of monotony
Scurrying by continuously piling onto the mainstream
Of mediocrity. Where is the dawning for philanthropy

CUNNING DIPLOMACY

There exists a point of numbness n' pain that you must
Endure; as you patiently stock up you modish defence
These exceptionally brash circumstances highlight the
Stark acerbic combatative backlashing pendulum stance

With empty bookshelves you stir up the rhetorical
Battleground of cunning diplomacy, vieing for the
Post graduate assurancy posing as a sophisticated
Informative cacophony exuding a synthesis derived

From an absurdly colourful philosophy while scrunching
Below menacing sarcasm of ineptly subdued pleasantries
Perving down on the fusty lighelad building into the
Aluminum metal trough as the highminded clown doctors

Was clean their grubby little hands and wherewith beckon their
Seaweed scented clothes, delineating with proscribed incitement
Incorrigibly prosecuting a phenology of fluting substantiveness
As communing earlespenny noticeably eardrums it's capaciousness

CYBORG

You won't ever bleed red blood when i
Violently stab you right in the heart
You're savage ancestors were peanut brained
Primates that amply struggled in straw huts

The game which you now play is much more
Sinister real where life shuts with zeal
You're killing machine's methods are pre
Historic, but your tactics are locked in

Futuristic storage, the cyborg may seem quite docile
In appearance but specialize in human disappearance
You're heroic make up is malevolent as soon as dying
Becomes prevalent, it's the spirit of protest, which

You superexaltingly detest especially when you know
That you're the best there's no heightened mediation
Or deliberation for the compact computer generation
The banal standard deviation is killing quotation

Your state of the art defences positively neutralize
The diabolical offences, you never fail to deliver a
Quick shiver; forcefully supplanting a degree of fear
To whomever is near, there's a new virus in your gear

DECEIVABLY ASSERTIVE

Disenchantingly I try hurriedly pull away
But my feet are frozen, so I hesitantly stay
Your love was like a wild dead dog walking
And I felt like a madman shrewdly stalking

Something must be pulling us together, just like
The seaspray from the beach leaping up in stormy
Weather, my heart fluctuates like a soft feather
Jolting obscenities in our temperamental dilemma

Happiness is sadly in short supply as it slips us by
Work is conceivably acerbic and deceivably assertive
You're ego is like rutter, in the masthead shutter
Which integral isotope; specifically must you mutter

DELICATE PASSION

You're sweetly blushing as I run my wettish gelid
Fingers briskly down the sides of your naked back
It's the emotion ruffling beyond sheer heart attack
Your pristine skin is smoother than finest silk

Strangely enough, I crave this urge to suck your milk
Watching the ascending crescent moon is such a thrill
I get a rush from you, as you catch my contagious chill
You seem to bloat then silently choke very desertly dry

You need some new batteries in your exhausted power supply
In order to universally recharge yourself and fly sky high
In my caring lovable arms art of love, gently oozes by
With external ecstacy our delicate passion will surely fly

DRIPPING TEARS

You're nervy sunken eyebrows painfully reveal a
Certain misery; there's a sad sunset reflecting
From your eyes, as your jauntless face suggest
That you've travelled wearily for so far n' winds

You're love is still suspended in icy animation
But mu heart beats wildly, in fluid machination
I can't even fill up my car up in this situation
How could I unassumedly end up in this situation

The stereotyped parochial ideas strengthen my fears
The wretched tie has been gathering tense momentum
For upteen years, is there a doctrine of discipline
To alleviate all our shortcomings, n' dripping tears

DRY WINTER

In dry winter I rescued you
You were bored had little to do
Dead leaves danced as the wind blew them by
They tumbled from green to bitter dry

Even the black window kissed my check
As I dozed off to fast asleep
You're love was so awfully dry
It even caused my garden to die

There were no more clouds in the sky
All I had was lovely high
One dark morning I heard you say
You did not want me to stay

Quickly were no more clouds in the sky
One dark morning I heard you
You did not want me to stay

Running around without any clout or clue
I tried to find you, but you suddenly flew
You were bored had little to do

ENDLESSLY WEENING

You're mind spins like a chunk of a
Windmill, as the freshly tendersoft
Fluttering of air flows to your bed
Endlessly weening at your alter ego

Hurriedly you paddle backwards on
Your bike gasping for more oxygen
The clog newsreel footage becomes
Tantalizingly clear when you slip

Beneath the purly coloured fishtank
Cocktailed with grassy bales of hay
And unconsumed bottles of champagne
Festering it's uncanny awkward vein

Is there much more to you than this
Melancholy refrain? I'm not so sure
That I have to register insane! Can
I drive out from this quagmire rain

ETERNAL BAIL

Mystical and magical you gently came to me
And swept my face with you're fresh breeze
Clouding my eyes in you're soft naked stream
Appearing so bright by been altruistic green

Soul cleansing me with a chirpy rigorous whiffle
The mystical and magical charming gaze befell me
This natural awesome aura stunned me into oblivion
Just for a faint while an renewed my upbeat style

Such catchy cuteness has serenaded me into sweetness
You're delectable kiss has stunned me into faintness
In a web of sudden anger you shrewdly ended it all
The humble beginning of my prosperous eternal ball

FAITH IN LIFE

Climb that mountain to the top
When you reach it you will see
All there is to feel, and more
When you conquer the big mountain
You shall drink from the fountain

Have faith in yourself; in your friends
Faith in every single thing that you do
With faith in life all things are nice
You shall see n' feel a brighter world
So share your faith around the world

FINGERBITTEN DISGUST

You're shambolic emotions are galvanized with
Fingerbitten disgust; as you try propitiate
A shamefaced autopsy about nervous potshot love
How can I grab your intense, vipassana attention

When you virescently slip past the latest detention
Your brain sinks deeply like a blown ballast shipper
Drunkenly dancing to the shindy music nightcap slipper
You can achieve your goal when you deceive the skipper

FIXATED PSYCHOSIS

Your like a rising storm in my life
Cutting me with the edge of a knife
Must I sit in silent anger and rage
Unsociably you slit me with a craze

Your eyes are sparkling silver red
As you're braved all that was said
There's a seldom seen rapture of glorious joy
Hidden in a mindswept gully of harmonious coy

When tripping subtely underneath the fixated psychosis
The psyche is empowered with self actualizing hypnosis
Incoherently; you cannot afford to run and hid when your
Inconsequentially in the unholy sights of the devil's eye

FOCUS FURTHER

What is it that makes you think?
You cannot do what you want to?
It's just a silly Irate negative thought
Causing us to navigate in the wrong port

If we are to prevail then we must sail
Through the wretched hail, n' replenish
All the uncooperative ail, then we can
Trek on the buckling mountainous trail

If we aim our sights right then we
Can see past the bluish, green mould
We can overcome the gravitating fright
Because our hearts will be full of might

We must never think we cannot do what we
Are supposed to! We should do what we're
Meant to; we have to focus further, and break
Out of our tortoiseshell to do exemplary well

FOREVER STAY

24

You make me smile like no one else can
I treasure the time that I hold your hand
I wish to give all n' everything to you my dear
With you by my side, I simply have nothing to fear

You're all I ever think about, every night and day
I miss you so much especially when you're far away
In my cuddlesome arms I hope you forever stay
So come along sweetly, and play with me today

FRUITY DREAM

You're like a wounded fleshy animal
That's just been pelted in the back
You left threatened, n' under attack
Don't run to me with your sorrowful

Pity! While scuttling for heavenly love
N' ditty; kissing oyster crustacean lips
In the festive season of wine and mirth
The universe reveals a renaissance birth

You jump up like a brand new unused appliance
An will never be able to study rocket science
If I don't learn from this incredible adventure
Then I'd hid behind the dynamic masked avenger

This episode is promptly coming to a close
And I'm only as good as what I can propose
I wish to seek refuge in your fruity dream
Scrambling for love n' virtuous self esteem

FUSTY VIRUS

I'm embarking on a strange journey to another land
Maybe it's somewhere in fable or a scientific scam
As I encroach upon a distant timely foreign sand
My entire body is swallowed up by the cool crisp

Mysterious foggy mist, I suppose you get the gist
This stormy night keeps vehemently clutching gist
Grip on me; my courage is the only armour I can see
This frightening situation isn't where I wish to be

The dark shadowy forest has unleashed it's hounds
As your footprints pounce down on the muddy swamp
There's a scenic filter which you track and stomp
Only to be obliterated in a senseless frenzy romp

The waxing moon disguises the lustful fusty virus of the
Chilly forest night etching upon a faint Neolithic light
Droplets of water gather then dampen my once dry clothes
Frosty nights have befallen on my slumbering patchy woes

GRANDIOSE HOSTILITIES

As the sun slowly sinks behind the willows
You're face lies burrowing, in the pillows
An hour later you shudder sleepy out of bed
Heroically refreshed, your inorganic nature

Is accustomedly swallowed up by the elegiac singing
Soprano opera night, there's an implied selectivity
Begging to be filled, in a sanely progressive light
The authoritative secularist figure shuns the empty

Impermeable space, trying to stick together calcerousy
Deposits with resorcinol glue; there's an exclusionary
Clause to the licentious disserment n' ethnographically
Couched epistemic disintegrating libelous disapproval

The euchronic accountability has lost it's unshakable agility
Astonishingly analogous is the bremping grandiose hostilities
Incongruously miling thru inadvertent curfews n' disconcerting
Flashbacks of embezzling live electrified corrupt mercenaries

GRANITE FINGERTIPS

Keyboard! The grandeur of splendour, gushes
Profusely from your pale granite fingertips
As you bounce off your ego trips. In the small
Seedy hours there's a genre of belatedly happy

Buzzing hips, impeccable tips, nescience clips
Why should you eat food from contaminated dips
Do you know what you have and what your losing
Don't risk it because it's not worth confusing

There are distractions which you may consider amusing
Rejoice in the things that you're accustomed to using
We all know that your in; an elite league of your own
And your pale granite fingertips don't belong at home

GURGLING DOWN THE DRAIN

I wish to catch my dreams. Before they
Fly off into space; my bones belong in
A prehistoric place scattered by years
Of neglecting burgeoning run down pace

There is much history behind the myth
Which is passed down by the sages lip
Even the pirates plundered and slit!
Where is the love? Where is the pit?

I am not one to moan or cheaply condone
I should take out an interest free oan
Maybe I need to whip myself into action
Because standing still, has no reaction

Come an feed my brain with a new strain
Please take aim n' stalk some fresh game
I cannot succumb to this whimsical fame
I feel like I'm gurgling down the drain

HEAVY CHAINS

The ghosts of your forefathers
Still carry their heavy chains
Rattling above embellishing pains
Burgeoning so frighteningly close

And destabillising our sacred hosts
No greater sacrifice is to be made
Or any higher ransom to be paid
All that we seek is to be saved

The voyage to freedom is just a fraction away
The plasms of the gods is like poetry in play
Recited over years of heroic deeds in displays
Our heavy chains must be sold, without slaves

IMPERILLING DUALITY

There was a concurrent lapse of arguable syntax
Protruding into my gap toothed, open wide mouth
As you briefly winded my exalting emotions, the
Unscrupulously groomed devoid of ethnicity male

Was hinting of an under the counter backroom sale
Our resourceful vintage purveyor was precociously
Yet meticulously drifting in the sea of anonymity
As he rescinded at the unkempt future monied mood

Nothing fancied was ordered from his penthouse room
There must be an unraveling hypotheses germinating
Beneath your unthinkably touchy imperiling duality
You're love life smooches with broods of sensuality

IMPREGNABLE COCOON

You've locked yourself in a totally isolated vicinity
Without any movable agility awkwardly reeling ashamed
Indefensibly cowering in a state of delayed shock as you
Carefully conceal the hidden scars, and invisible wounds

In you're impregnable cocoon; yet you feel downtrodden like a
Bafoon! Can you still afford to eat with a shiny silver spoon
The shackles of anonymity will hopefully be unchained real soon
And you shall be released for this barbarous torturous platoon

HOLLOW STILLNESS

Your once fruitful green paddock is becoming arid dry
In a desperate bid to seek out some greener pastures
You quickly stumble by, the breastplate of courage
Repels the poison darts thrown by the hidden enemy

Your like the never satisfied spoilt shopaholic! Contemporary
Consumer novice continuously upgrading their bargain hunting
Competitive capacity and unquenchable appetite for the latest
Non lasting energy efficient, use by date renewable products

Nefariously your choking the air supply from my pithy throat
Needles to say, I enjoy the calmness of you're silky breath
And the hollow stillness of your reciprocal intriguing depth
You must always empathetically watch where you greedily step

HOMEGENIC HEART

I wish to soar higher than the peaceloving winless dove
And expose the blistering hurt to a caring soul up above
I feel the passion emanating from you're homogenic heart
And the sound of voodoo drums, beating wildly in the hot

Climaxing Caribbean sun blinding my face as I stealthily
Pause to examine my sorrowful case, because our personal
History may never be written on any facebook or computer
Page. However I have sorted to incorporate my complexing

Rages your universalistic outlook is surpressed with age
Like noctilucent clouds in the sky we condemn the brazen
Infirmity. I beg for solitude before I flee to outer space
May I seek exemption from this pitiless hostile human race

IMPERTURBABLY CRUDE

There are no more haunted lovers
In this cold dark ancient castle
What existed once is now all gone
Our heuristic methods shall leave

No stone unturned, regardless of
How immutably they may disappear
"There's a somber impalpable feeling
In this once torturous, stone relic

It/s so imperturbably crude, maybe we
Should walk away n' leave them to play
The haunting spirits must be left to rest
Even though we try to valiantly repossess

IMPRESSIVELY PRESSURED

I'm frantically running, first past the post
Your always rushing about outlandishly brash
With unfriendly climes centrally bowdlerized
Figuratively within lumpen faced expressions

Your gutted voice lies impressively pressurized
And lays perceptively scandalised. Is there any
Concealed artifacts or confiscated contraband in
The rickety worn out heavily guarded luggage bag

If so, then we can rejuvenate whatever is sluggish
Why be such a clumsy boring brat? When your suited
To rise above the pack! You can afford to dress as
Much smarter than that dancing on a silhouette mat

IMPETUOUS KICKBACK

Your eyes sparkle like a thousand
Mirrors reflecting from the sun
Have you ever seen two rainbows
Pleasantly colliding into one

Can we run into the fiery eclipsing sun
With the euphoria of love, just for fun
Life delineates us many arduous challenges
Some things unite us; yet others divide us

It's like you're singing old songs
In some trendy up market café
Songs of hope with emotional scope
That sting you by they're ray

Speedily you descend deeper underground
To escape the predatory dinosaur attack
Which is launching it's impetuous kickback
Be careful not to blow you're hollow stack

INACCESSIBLY REDUCED

After such punishing competition, you're still
Tumbling forwards, simultaneously drawing from
Pithy smooth silkiness of eye watering victory
As hip hugging friends are duopoly refashioned

You've explicitly chosen carefully scripted words
Infusing cultural nuances in diplomatic tactility
The wedgy goals are direct an frustratingly inept
Your impeccable credentials are character checked

Within these cathedral walls, there's a coursing growL
Acrimoniously bespattered an swoothing boosterishly as
The coverextended imbalances are intimidately produced
Those absolutist subsidiaries are inaccessibly reduced

INFINITELY BUBBLING

The boiling molten lava in my tactile mind is
Infinitely bubbling like your windswept pride
It's gushingly fuming and tactfully consuming
Bellowing it's sunny, fondly reminiscing

Fractured by gone days, life has become twisted
Like a kink, the rope is snapping at every wink
I'm overhauling the collaborating mentorship of
Your sordid ego trip; with it's snozzling trick

The mounted glovebox is comparatively pedestrian at
Where I bask, your unmistakable laugh rests frosted
Behind the mirrored windscreen glass. Will you drink
Like a thirsty alcoholic from the manufactured cask?

INNUMERABLE ROUTINE

There must be a certain, sacred place
Where I can heal my afflicting wounds
If not, then I'll sadly sulk, so marooned
I'm sick of all those sleazy topless bars

With their stench of alcohol, n' Havana cigars
All those side show kicks and sexy striptease
Matinee flicks only reveal their scummy tricks
I wish I could conduct some alternative energy

So as to revive my alabaster sourpass face
Which is bent severely in and out of place
I'm not a throw away rug even though I'm buried
Undug; a notion may seldom come that I can plug

I must remain sheltered in my space, because
An overwhelming anxiety is thrown at my face
Our lives keep turning like a rusty wheelbarrow
A sad innumerable routine which makes us serene

INSPIRING SPONTANEITY

I want to take you on a voyage so far away
Of inspiring spontaneity to unknown places
Where sweet n' mellow love clearly embraces
I wish to speak openly with my happy heart

Then murmur away all my insecurities an sordid
Frustrations, and leave the web of lies behind
We need to learn to live and love with a purpose
An trek out the route without a slippery surface

INVARIABLE ANALYSIS

There's a repressively mnemonic victimization
Maxzimising the tyranny within my choking soul
I feel so awfully drained wreacking pain from
The numb cul de sac of incomplete fulfillments

Condemning illusions and unhelpful treatments
Do I need a new prescription for my ailments
What sermon can unlock my neurotic inhalents
The invariable analysis is highly calculable

Unerring blind choices from the unending curiosity
Sparkling in a wineglass vacuum of escape velocity
Forever silenced, with prudish metabolic ferocity
Why is it so compelling to receive any generosity

IWALANI

I'm sucking on a delicious pineapple
Amidst the hot tropical coconut moon
Your irradescent eyes fire up like a
Panther's sigh as you lay semi naked

In the steamy Hawaiian, lazy afternoon
Skinny dipping in a gurgling rock pool
Next to a bubbling lava bed of melting
Mud breathing the humidity with a thud

Your more mysterious and bewitching than any
Eclipsing of Saturn's colossal pinkish moons
Which leaves my senses revving like a mustang
An twitching like a baboon! Iwalani a goddess

Must have given you your unique name because I've
Never ever heard of another quite the lovely same
You're Polunesian hair carries a string of Tahiti
With cellulose orchid black; an illustrious stack

The vibrant sensuality you project, gyroscopes my pounding
Heart into streams of mountainous cloudy crystal clean air
My melancholy mind spins upwards like a gigantic whirlwind
Will you read me a bedtime story as you brush my wet hair

Upon your koa built bed or sing me a lullaby instead
Can I make you an invigorating soft mokokai cocktail
Overlooking the volcanic ash, from our penthouse pad
Feasting on a seafood smorgasbord on our balcony mad

Just as I'm thumbling with imagination's pain
I hope all of the effort isn't wasted in vain
I'll be going back to Honolulu a little strange
Iwalani, should I feel like I'm short of change

LAMENTING BRAIN

You're like a wounded angry owl
That's eager to scratch n' growl
As the nightwind turns to prowl
Will you harvest you're plough?

You're love is like the stirring
Whispering waters which flow out
Into the unchartered treacherous sea
An I always yearn to be alone free

Thus breaking the stubborn shackles which
Dull and torment my tired lamenting brain
I only seek to relieve the delusional strain
Is there any antidote for this viperous pain

LISTEN N' PAUSE

Whenever I'm sad you make me laugh out loud
So I can't understand why you're feeling so
Let down; you instill a positive hope n' joy
Into my miserable, boring, dreary existence

As you diligently try to keep me out of strife
I can't wait for the day for you to be my wife
Pragmatically you adhere to my simple, needy cause
Once in a while, I have to sit down listen n' pause

LOVE IS THE ANSWER

Love is like magic
And it always will be
For love still remains
Life's sweet mystery
Lave works in so many ways
That are wondrous strange
Thus there's nothing in life
Which love, cannot change!
Love can transform
The most commonplace
Into beauty' splendor
And sweetness and grace
Love is unselfish
Understanding and kind
For it sees with its heart
And nor with it's mind
Love is the answer
That everyone seeks
Love is the language
That every heart speaks
Love does turn the magic key
Which reveals life's mystery
Love can't be bought or sold
It's priceless, forever free

LUCKY STARS

I thank my lucky stars they sent you to me
For you and I were just always meant to be
We have a bond that's too strong to break
We share a love that no one else can take

With you I feel a comfort so warm and happily true
My soul is gently filled with bubbling sedated you
Every time I see you my heart suddenly skips a beat
You make my life sparkle and so pleasantly complete

LULLING TEARS

I don't seek to plagiarise you're ideas
Or steamroll the bohemian lulling tears
I don't wish to diffuse your hurting angst
Or cause a whirlpool in your bulging pants

Maybe we can crawl around like giant hungry ants
Especially when you take off your sweating pants
I never got to kiss, the sweetest lips in town
Because you were too busy to consider me round

I may not be the greatest guy that's ever been
But you have never witnessed, what I have seen
As I watch the three quarter moon turning full
I can imagine feeding you in the swimming pool

Imperatively we glimpse into the fascinating sequence
Of positive thought with an overriding skepticism we
Exemplify the reverberating indulgent schisms, whilst
Excavating the fossil red remains in your mon logical
Hub of dissatisfied reasonigs, with reducible concerns
And insufficient importance; stemming from hypothetical
Unreliable sources we need to listen to some new voices
We must try to change the pessimistic for the realistic

AESTHETICS	Is the theory of art and beauty
EPISTEMOLOGY	Is the theory of human knowledge
ETHICS	The theory of human conduct ' morals
EXISTENTIALISM	A doctrine saying man is responsible only to himself
LOGIC	The theory of accurate thinking \ and reasoning
LOGICAL POSITIVISM	A concept stating that without practical effects theories Are simply meaningless
ONTOLOGY	The notion of what does really exist as opposed to what Appears to exist
PRAGMATISM	The ideology that knowledge is an instrument of action
SCEPTICISM	The idea that everything open to doubt
SOLIPSISM	The idea that nothing exists but me and my mental states and my mental states The idea that the right action

produces the greatest happiness
Almighty is the faith that moves mountains
If we don't believe, then we won't achieve
With faith we can build a tower of Babel
An latch onto the heavenly cosmic cradle

Wiccar is the unholy pagan craft of the wise
Sneering ancient ties deducing mystical vies
Logical analysis may conform to simultaneous
Paralysis influenced with scientific malices

Psychology states we are what we think we are
The rationalists suggest I think therefore I am
Existentialism says a man is free to do whatever he can
Personally for myself I do say, I exist therefore I can

With so many varied examples of modern thought
Which proper method of thought do you support

MUSIC

"Music can be the everlasting joyful dreams
Of the shepherd's flute or the soft enchanting
Melody n' arousing feeling of vibrating string
And snappy rhythms, of notation creeping up on

Your feet resulting in some new exciting swing
Which makes you feel like a newly crowned king
Cheerful music gives you zeal so charmingly gay
Making you sway in a very stylish n' awkward way
Music is really something else; it enables us to Bang along to
the big bass drum with subdued hum
It rapturously instills it's happy touch of youth
If in doubt I'm ample proof; harried thoughts are

Briskly hurried away, exciting opera's are written
At night as well as day, refreshing backyard blues
Heavy metal riffs, swift pub rock beats, slick jazz
Licks are masterfully played slashing boredom's way

Scrupulous musician's have constantly maintained music
Sounds great when all instruments are grouped together
To undergo new weather in a harmonious melodious liner
What can be finer than Beethoven's symphony in B minor

NAKED DUMMIES

Your dwarfish character is blighted by hate
Then mixed in a gargantuan fatalistic state
No one seems to cross handedly relate to you
As your crystallized in smutty complications

Endowed with vexing limitations, we eagerly conduct
Some further succinct investigations as extract the
Futile observations, there's unspecified entrapments
That are tediously resistant to surmounting captions

Disentangled and unadorned naked dummies
Synergistically yearn for piles of cloth
While agonizing in diaphanous nightdress
Of the newly hatched nurturant burlesque

Garotting in a décolletage of stunning lashes
Stupendously slick and always so fuchsia neat
There is nothing more to reveal, because this
Tale is movingly brisk and littered with risk

NARROW LANEWAYS

Whilst strutting down the intriguingly broad
Boulevard filled with Imposingly magnificent
Architecture couple by ghastly gargoyle statues
I hurriedly stroll past the narrow laneways with

Graffiti covered red brick walls n' painted pipes
Into a sidestreet café adorned with tall fluxing
Glowing lightboxes, scented in lavender perfumed aroma
Therefore exhibiting the city's vibrant counterculture

There's an informal subtle décor brought to my attention
In the notion of soul searching n' often fond exploration
As I jostle amongst the hordes of people in this crowded
One way street, It's you that I desperately hope to meet

NO ONE ELSE WOULD EVER DO

I was putting plaster over the cracks on
My wall as you walked into the cold room
Then I knew that it was you and only you
Realistically; no one else would ever do

No one else even comes close to you
I just like the things that you tend to do
You're so sweet n' special that I love only you
And no one else could ever take the place of you

OBLITERATED PAST

Spiraling into the inner sanctum of nothingness
I'm propelled by a breadth of astrological burnt
Our matter; from the depths of oblivion shooting
In the mediocrity of earthly daily non existence

Very freshly graduating from the embryonic cocoon
Spawning a methodological sphere of cosmic raccoon
You flap your newly hatched wings n' gradually fly
As a monarch butterfly in the lower depths of the

Atmospheric sky; you seldomly flashback at you're
Obliterated past where you seemingly were such an
Expendable outcast. Is there any rhyme or reason
For us to dwell upon, the maligning silly season

ONGOING SCREAM

There's no agonizing love to be strewn along
The way; as steadily drive past the bleak
Arid desert, thru to the valley of the winds
There's more than one lost soul and a lonely

Ghost apologizing for their sins, they're locked
In purgatory, like a rusty nail in a rotting bin
There's an upcoming virulent which we must cross
And an ongoing scream that sounds like it's lost

PEDIGREE PEAKS

The angels must have made you in heaven
Then sent you down here on planet earth
To bestow upon us, a calm new age birth
Love unflutters with some protean mirth

Your sunny smile sparkles like spring birth
As you twinkle your chubby red juicy cheeks
Snug wisdom you empower from pedigree peaks
Evaporating the surface fog and wintery dew

Strolling thru icy meadows of rainbow hue
Whilst gathering flowers I patiently gaze
Into your eyes, listening to the chirping
Bluebirds, as you hint at some worthwhile

Cheerful surprise, impatiently I run out of
The forest green to catch up to you but you
Amusingly smiling wave down at me, gloating
Lofty on top of the angelic clouds so clean

PELICAN SUNRISE

I'm bell hopping around the streamlined seajetty
Peering mused on triangular dish sized jellyfish
As I wonder in amazement on this pelican sunrise
The babbling brook, crouches amongst ocean waves

The rustling of the leaves envelopes the icy cool
Breezy days, the lighthouse casts dark shadows as
I slippingly tumble downwards the greenish meadows
Like a clown in a circustent I freakishly vent and

The freakshow is to be enjoyed as the promoted main event
We must carefully try to circumvent, the anxious hellbent
Out of failure stems success, an out of fear arises hope

Yet sadly some of us are still far from been able to cope

PLEASURABLE CONTENT

I can feel the freshly painted polish from your
Fingernails; tingling onto my cold pressed skin
My organs are experimenting the heightened level
Of adrenalized excitement, then you continue to

Playfully arouse my tense frothing sensuality
I'm vaguely mesmerized in the kaleidoscope of
Accumulating and titillating sexual desire as
Your silly luscious lips grovel over my chest

When I gently stroke your pubic hair n' kiss
You're entire body with a passionate intent
We can reach a state of pleasurable content
I vie to make love to you for hours n' hours

Until we climax n' cool off in bubbly showers
One fiery night with you, makes up for years
Of abstinent neglect. When I look around I can
Honestly say that you're the one I will select

PLIANT SAPLING

There's an amount of reciprocal danger
Stoved away in this inscrutable manger
You're inner cravings have lapsed into a
Shuddering halt; waiting for you to bolt

It's so recognizably sad, when your so mad
Your life is like a pliant sapling in need
Of the next shovel full of nutrient earth
Continuously growing in a flowering birth

Your concluding imagination is seditious in thought
Thinly repercolating an administration courageously
Blocked; often ridiculed n' proclaimed securely locked
Extirpating a declared immersion of feelings unlocked

PSYCHO CITY

We're actually surfing upon the internet
The highway of the future is no tame pet
So roll the dice and place your last bet
This ain't no ego trip or thrilling kick

It's straight in your face, cyberspace quick
Why do we have to sip from the hardware chip
We all wear the number of the horrible beast
In the computer feast: this electronic gizmo

Gadgetry is extracted from refuge sub human yeast
There's no way out, only pessimistic fear n' doubt
Why trance around in joe boxers, like a kickboxer?
The bigger they are then the harder they will fall

But you have to drop them first, then have a ball
Amid all of the commotion we tend to shed emotion
Like an android, desperately needing locomotion
The wolves are not at bay if you choose to stay
The indulging claws seem weepish upon bloody floors
Maybe we should knock harder on silent closed doors
Dealers, stealers, hookers, sookers, pimps, whimps
High society low life variety all in it's entirety

They're all testament of the scoundrel witty
Regardless of age, power or the nitty gritty
We're all clones of this hungry, crazy kitty
So welcome to the demoralizing, psycho city

PULSES OF PANIC

Antagonistically you shuffle your hands up in the air
Sympathetically I sense a maladjustment hovering bare
Such an unfulfilled desire wallowing nakedly in shame
Your collaboratively entrenching goals are sadly lame

Catalyzing an exploitable diffracting mindset openly
Culminating in a progressing seclusion of deplorable
Stellar gain; queasily indentured in a slightly stoic
Frame, fleetingly curbing the propagating disastrous

Flame, as you cross the river you jump onto a faster
Horse but that drags you way off course. An abstract
Occurrence as populations are mercilessly slaughtered
Like innocently herded incarcerated sheep, there are
Pulses of panic, on the radar bleep!

PUNCTUATING SADLY

My heart is intolerably gushing and punctuating sadly
My brain is impudently excruciating n' grappling madly
You're rectractable responding sigh, cutely offers me
A tangible goodbye; with overdone eyelashes and lips

And a wickedly naughty, see through black negligee
You're accurate reminder fashionably calls me over
Neutralizing the ratiocinating developing misnomer
Recapitulating for the dreaded battlefield of life

There is no facilitating support, only an insignificant
Train of thought; paralyzing my verve to humbly succeed
Your like a mermaid calmly swimming in the gigantic sea
Signaling the dolphins to be free; what a sight to see

RAKISH RETREAT

You're like a big war hero
Which cannot rest in peace
Reeming as a soul deceased
You wish your life is transferable

But quiver when it's so unbearable
There's no new insertable rakish retreat
Your passion turns from mighty gladiator
To a euphemistical; aggressive spectator

Your muscles look like they've been
Mashed together in a coffee grinder
What a feeble tymphonic crash as you
Violently smash all the thrifty cash

RARE EMOTION

The whole world feels so very new
As your love fills my joyous soul
There is laughter in my cloudy eyes
Because I'm not afraid of good byes

The summer clouds keep passing by
Without a droplet of cooling rain
There's a moisture beneath my sheet
With a trickle of nervous cold feet

I'm not afraid to cross the ocean deep
Because I'm excited with calming sleep
There's an influx of loyal, rare emotion
Adrenalizing our state of sheer devotion

RESPLENDENTLY BELLOWING

There's a wonderful flutter in the put of my stomach
Resplendently bellowing like a moistened sprinkling
Delicate thunderstorm, marvelously twinkling over
Our damp somnolent perfumed garden where elongated

Sunlight illuminedly flitters, richocheting
Off the galvanized scaffolding underneath a
Vague scrumpy aurora sky; the flapping wings
Of our souls constantly transliterate n' back

Pedal, like medieval cartwheels in queer whir
Stirring up images of the intersection in our
Lives. I happily yearn for the security of your arms
And the peace n' tranquility, of you're loving charms

RESTLESS SPIRIT

The furiously reinvigorated rebellion is
Contentiously pillaging; unplugging it's
Restless spirit in retaliation for such
Extempore exasperation of hyprocrisy gone

Mad, there's concentrating departure
Simmering without a justifiable reason
Deteriorating in strained abandonment
From subjugated consistant hamperings

You're psyche has sunk into the potholes of
Sheet disgust; so whom can you openly trust
Your mind has shrunk in the bottomless well
Your life is bleeding, but who can you tell

ROLLING IN MUD

You're love has filled me up with so any
Wonderful feeling I jibe like I'm flying
In a hot air balloon under the summery moon
As u filter thru the bottleneck of previous

Tense emotions I now avoid the petty commotions
Like wild horses banging they're heads together
In the chilly forest night, I am full of fright
Trying to reach a plateau of prosperity n' might

Peering up into the lonesome planets and darkly lit bluer
Galactic skies; I'm staring at you thru the bicycle spokes
Wondering when you're going to choke! Are you as happy as a
Pig rolling in mud? Can I slap your face with a giant thud?

ROUTINELY CALLOUS

Like the flappable platypus and the gasping goose
I'm chuckling hysterically like a bullnosed moose
You're doubting the validity n' smudging authenticity
Spaciously gracious, are those garnt washed up faces

There's no ranting n' raving just pure misbehaving
Don't need intriguing scheming or naïve dreaming
I'm not routinely callous or neurotically jealous
I shall propose a toast for the heartrending host

The unpredictable cocktail of art and party mixes well
Into the flavours of the anecdotal sinister and crafty
You're frivolous persuasions are loquacious abrasions
Respondingly you rush to tag along, so enjoy the party

SAPLENT SEDUCTRESS

Our saplent seductress beckonly observes
The finicky horde of mesmerized disciples
Who crave at her scantling voluptuous frame
But wallow with sarcocystic protuberant pain

And the mountainous sulphuric inner shame
Skullduggery is so irrepressibly disarming
Prospelytizing n' analyzing what is charming
Setting a precedent with a caveat alarming

I'm sick of sleazy blame n' lazily lame
Mystery and mystique are my major game
I'm a wild child that will never be tame
In all of my adventures, what did I gain

SATURN SKIES

72

I felt the soft aurora borealis flicker
Thru the dark moon as my windswept face
Trombones from the compounding alarm of
Saturn skies, there's a mystique that's

Fragile n'' deep, echoing the ancient nymphs
A mutating oasis portrays a convalent bond
Fluttering upon stellar rainbows and inter
Galactic clouds, punctually swirling around

Acoustically dancing n' fluttering in albedo Capricorn mist
Displaying itself like a flattened yellow disk, floundering
Saturn skies mesmerize with a gravitational planetary charm

SCUPPERED PSYCHOSIS

There's an enthused theatricality while
You display you're lachrymose witticism
Whilst vacating the scuppered psychosis
Pertaining from the truncated obsession

Such anthemic timbales categorically
Play so weirdly; the botulistic beat
Confrontingly sad ancillary abeyance
A strange spectacular ebullient feat

You smartly brown coloured wingtipped shoes
Are set to entice the precise business views
What group dynamics receive any social support
Like members of the chess club all above board

SILVER CHALICE

You're eyes penetrate deep into my weary bones
Like the sultry stingy, humid night desert air
Crisply frisking onto my sweat soaked embroided
Cotton shirt and torn floral silky pastel pants

As the sand becomes covered with marauding ants
I still intend to locate the long lost mythical
Enchanted royal place then we shall toast from
The ruby laddened, mystical meek silver chalice

The corridors are aligned with the scent of enticing
Jasmine myrrh an honeywax, and the streamlined paths
Glitter from the huge reflecting golden chandeliers
The fortress walls are paved with mudbrick an stone

The mighty cedar palace gates are opened only by the
King's oarsmen; in the surrounding moat fastlt drink
The shepherd's goat, the moonlight flickers n' soothes
Our restless souls, the cobbled streets are filled by

The holiest of men, preaching they're values and wise
Doctrines in many indecipterable and hypnotic tongues
Whilst peddlers barter they're wares in the market place
Merchants offer bargains at a reduced semicircular space

To sell and exchange exotic gifts with tender grace
Wise old men pass down unimaginable myths n' legends
Interesting fables and stories of perilous heroic glories
To generations new, that's a skill acquired only by a few

Subtle aroma's quietly escape from the chimney's flue
Oil filled shining lamps expel some rare incence clue
With my beating heart I madly fell in love n' promise

No one else can caress my heart, then split it in two
No one else is as pure and as sweet as delightful you
Like the ascending crescent moon n' brightly lit stars
We were made for heaven, traveling express thru Mars

SINISTER RIFT

Amongst the smouldering hysteria of unrepentant quarreling
Mutilated by the portals of death; surfaced a buccaneering
Slouchingly weltering generosity the spirits macarbly call
You're name, condensing with an infanticide ferocious game

What secrets lurk behind these unholy darkening shadows
Begrudging their rattling bones in the choked graveyard
Overlooked by rusty corrugated iron n' chimney flues
Are we wisened enough to destroy all the evil dues?

Thirsty wild dogs howl incessantly with blood stained teeth
The full moon shines pyroclastically impatient on it's trip
We cannot afford to inherit the bitterly slug haunting gift
Returning from darkness let's annihilate this sinister rift

SPIRALING CREVICE

Banqueting on the spiraling crevice of your
Inner sanctum; my stomach suddenly squirmed
With outstretched arms I furiously ambushed
The cunningly cool, wispy faced battlechief

Though our torrid encounter was unrefinably annoying
Narrowly twisting n' sputterly yanking at the dullish
Imperfection of the interminttently high stone walled
Quay, the indivisible squirearchy idolaters apyingly

Peep, as normal folk seldom weep! Is the world at your feet?
My soul has been flattered; but I stikk turn the other check
What secrets do you store n' keep, surely you on another peak
I'm humble and meek! I have adapted so I am not entirely week

STILL SHIVER

Apprehensively I smittingly glide past your
Bureaucratic smile then I try to crack thru
The ponderous receptacle from empty icyness
My anklecaps are swamped in slimy soggy mud

It's raining heavily on the other side of the river
That's causing us to shuffle and shriekingly quiver
All alone but not dethroned I race to the snowcapped
Mountains n' I still shiver. Is there any deliverance

From this monolith pillar or only a bottomless chiller?
Meteorically uneventful rises, this suspenseful thriller
When can you change my pattern of preconceived thoughts
So I can victoriously stand proud and sincerely deliver

SUBJECTIVE REFLECTIVES

I'm drying my soaking wet socks in the middle
of the night in front of the fire and waiting
for you to walk right in n' lift me even higher
there's a cosmic spacey hue fructifying in the

Night; Ineffably breezing between a disgruntled
Consternation. It's such an offensive situation
Gradually frazzled with concentrated flirtations
Irreconcilably necktied by haphazard innovation

There are no insubordinate presumptions or any
Inconspicuous reflective when confronted with
Subjective receptive and explicit reflectives
what designated interventions befit objectives

SUCCINT EMBRACE

You're baffling gaze, befalls the surreal twist
As I approach you in the battling twilight mist
Your bittersweet eyes embark a succinct embrace
Offering a kiss to warm, your frostbitten hands

Then hovel over you're freezing brindled body
There cannot be any form of erroneous mistake
Because too much importance; is here at stake
You stultify your standardized storiated take

You're always late, so how do you fairly rate
Will you get irate, when dinner is served on
A barbeque plate, who looks at what you've eaten
Must I gargle to flush out this sorrowful state

SUPPLICATING EGO

You're supplicating ego is landing upon ghostly
Wings embedded with acute humiliating vengeance
Sneeringly acclimatizing by destructive coercion
Whilst battling the demons in your frigging mind

You're heart hasn't got the correct fortitude and
Your brain lacks the momentum to advance you sane
Because it's plagued with rusty gears, which have
Not been oiled for many years, your soul has been

Battered, as a result of all those turbulent fears
Your in desperate need of some healing an soothing
Cloud resting peace, yet your penance is overdrawn
And thwart by so many strange and perilous disease

SWAMPY MOONLIGHT

There's an increasingly heavy weight to carry
Upon you're tender shoulders, as you scramble
Downwards from the slippery sandstone boulders
Your eyes keep squinting at the sparkling rays

Breezing onto torrid running glistening waters
Hurriedly wiping the cold sweat from your brow
Bewildered you moan like a famished jersey cow
Even when I walk on the peaceful falling snow

I feel like I'm swimming over a tropical waterfall
Caressed by the soft magic of the swampy moonlight
Locked in the hardy throes of sweet revving emotion
Our love was so wondorous n' full of weird commotion

TANGLED SHOES

I've lied to you and I've lied
To myself, I drifted and shifted
From things that I thought I loved
I'm so overwhelmed with grief n' pity

When I walk around this cold empty city
My feet feel like cement in tangled shoes
My tongue speaks wrangled of yesterday's news
Could you offer me a room, with clearing view?

TEMPESTUOUS TEMPERAMENT

You yell like a poor begotten ancient with
That is just about to be burnt at the stake
You're red eyes look like dark cave openings
As you hurriedly run screaming from the loud

Persecuting gun, in front of the village fountain
You were justly cornered then savagely surrounded
Your sour trenchant wit reflected words of anguish
Redividing the delicacy of tempestuous temperament

Fizzing in an overstimulated despicable mountain
Of myth; raggedly terrifying and nullifying thus
Loquaciously exemplifying, your vulnerable emotion
Acrimoniously exhibiting an unpredictable devotion

THE AGONY OF BROKEN SPIRITS

Lost in a world of rotating anger
Laughter torments my ghostly soul
Passion deeply runs inside the bodies
Of those, who grin at what would have

Imminently imagined to be purely bold
The leaves are clinging to the ground
They have nowhere else to gently fall
Like battered pebbles on the seashore

We dissolve they're right to evolve
What of reality? It plagues my mind
As it has done, from centuries past
Willows weep n' sing their sad songs

Sighing at your sundrenching eyes, which
Lay a curse upon lonely evaporating lips
Reflecting the agony of broken spirits, you're
Cheerful charm howls like the everlasting wind

THE BREEZE OF YOUR MUTE ECHO

You made my imagination confounded n' confused
After you left me upon that clamourous sound
I still felt the breeze of you're mute echo
Pushing my naive loneliness over the cliff

As I tripped into that slimy sluggish gutter
Of raw jealousy and tempestuous selfish hate
Below where I feel onto the stage of the world
Was an endless assortment of dryish characters

Wanting more and taking more thus leaving
Me with less than my share of envy n greed
My blood boiled, when I tasted that bread
Of stale mouldy words whose promises bled

THE REAL DEAL

In life we're constantly searching for
That elusive, special little something
A thing that makes us fly without wings
When I close my eyes every single night

All I see is this warm wondorous sight
That thing that I wish to touch n' hold
That is truly more precious than silver or gold
This entity which engulfs all my hopes n' dreams

It helps me perceive how love should be
It straightens me up; before I slide
And always dries my tears when I cry
It will be my best n' loyalist friend

Who will sincerely be there till the very end
It's not so complicated to try and comprehend
There's nothing in this world that I'd rather
Feel, than to be in love in love with, the real deal!

THIRSTY STRAWS

It's such a tiring, massive chore
Shopping at the big department store
It's not a waste to enhance your taste
You resent the haste but try new paste

You don't know me: n' I really don't know you
If you choose to know me then it's up to you
When someone looses do we incur the bruises?
When I need a kiss, will you give me a miss?

Or reward me with more, succulent sweet bliss
Let's compare the notes n' evaluate the quotes
There's truly no assurance for your endurance
Are you still facilitating or just clambaking

It's so void to be paranoid: we must penetrate
The cause to exonerate the clause, then we can
Meditate the flaws and pacify, the hungry claws
So we can quench, the raucously thirsty straws

TORTURED EGO'S

I'm frittering uncomfortably in a cool bewildered nest
My mind is foundering intangibly like a stalking pest
My heart is repeatedly pivoting from the lucent mess
Our feet keep shuffling in the mild senectitude rest

We cannot realistically remain sentimentally attached
When all of the dire stakes are very unjustly patched
Our love needs a critical analysis before it's botched
Our speechless tongues and tortured ego's still try to

Facilitate the frustrating numbness which is bestowed
Upon us, without any dignity but inglorious propriety
There's such an unfair component in this reluctant game
Which heavily bleeds us unfathomably deep and so insane

TRANQUIL LULLNESS

There's an intimate friendship promulgated by
Our anticipating strategic alliance; we're so
Gobbled up by the feuding deviance, n' eagerly
Absconding to the grim disconnected reliance

There's a subtle whisper in the night appeasing
A ghostly light, the tendril of life becomes to
Crippling rife; causing a tranquil lullness while
Encrypting out missionary sight n' visionary light

When you're weary cagey body loses it's battle to
Survive, there's a remainder embedded in your cry
Can you forgive the wasted promises; nervously spoken
How do you conceal the scapegoated unforgivable token

TRAUMATIC CONVULSIONS

You look like you're taking a shower
With your raincoat on; as you murmur
The darkest hour is just before dawn
But your life is encased like a pre-

Historic fossilized stone! There's a seedy
Side to love when it's sundried like burnt
Mud, frothing from the bubbling lava pit
You graciously stumble, amongst the slit

How can you have such a protracting iron grip
When it's neglected like a damaged bloody lip
There is a resounding abnormally loud tirade
Boded like some incautiously apoplectic raid

Solvency is quick remedy for congenial conjunctions
How often would you attend these worn out functions
Posed by drawn our elements with petty injunction
Have you alleviated the post traumatic convulsions

TWENTY LONG YEARS

It's been well over twenty long years
Since I first kissed your tender lips
It brought so much tantalizing bliss
Then I still remember the quirky way

You used to comb you're silky, fairy hair
In the stillness of the moonlit airy night
Urging me to walk in form the foggy light
Can you still kiss me the same way tonight

An rejuvenate the passion of our yesterday
It's so inspiring, watching you chanelling
All the power that you withhold inside
Maybe we can go on a magic carpet ride

UNCEASINGLY BURNS

My blackened hear is frequently kindling
My famished desire is converting the fire
As the flame inside me unceasingly burns
The moment of detonation miserably yearns

I ask now for all my sulking to disappear
Unwrapping the wailing turns and pleasant
Thoughts of yesteryear. I'm reaching for the
Sunblest skies n' dispensing with the alibi's

My life feels like a decongested dry cough
My throat is swollen n' constantly flems up
Is there an imminent release from this stuff
Why does fate keep on tormenting me so much?

UNCEREMONIOUSLY CAPSULATED

Lazily I chase the solitude for my unholy dream
The angels are singing to me as I loudly scream
A vague hollow emptiness filters the thick coldsweep
Constricting my soul with desist emotionless comfort

Fleshless bones hungrily search for added rotting meat
They're hunger moans unsuppressedly invigorated in the
Starveling chest; strange hypnotic tunes wither oneiric
Memories of deceased mortals unceremoniously capsulated

Within a timeless world, picture framed in between the plump
Interdisciplinary tattletale connection thwarting the severe
Thuggee inception. There's an onerous taskmaster as I stampede
Over the moisty riverbed, searching for a shed to rest my head

UNHOLY FIST

The jaws of darkness are slowly loiting
Into my flesh, they're teeth marks keep
Piercing through my narrow brittle bones
So it's needless to throw anymore stones

The howling of the night is rapidly closing
It's vexing unholy fist over my entire body
Trawling in the vast echelons of unworldly safe
There comes a time to administer a worthy faith

Can this planet survive, with so much constant neglect
Feminine, pollution, deforestation, and global warming
And the brainwashed fertilizing armies of perpetual hate
Fear not! There's a messiah coming to alleviate our fate

UNINHABITABLE PSYCHE

Is there an opulent, administrative department
Or an accessibly viable comforting compartment
Excellence is undeniably unattainable in this life
Everything is uninhabitable in you're split psyche

If only there was a classical figure securely locked
Between your harmoniously copious contemporary being
Just an abstract figure of something which has been
I'm not all deluded by your uninhabitable psyche

Where's the myths and the exquisite mother of pearl gifts
Only the left over neglected monuments produce such rifts
Introspective analysis vaguely concludes with hitherto paralysis
Nonsensory thought is distinct reflection of natural selection

UNPRETENTIOUS LOVE

97

As I sit bare chested on the mountain slope
Watching the yellowy orange sinking sun dip
Into the nightly; rising banana shaped moon
Suddenly you creep out of the shaded woods

An into my arms bringing me much comfort n' toy with
You're rosy cheeks n' sweet faced unpretentious love
You're like a long lost; humble separated companion
Pouting your lips onto my raised up edgy erect ears

Effortlessly kissing me behind the point of my neck
Whilst tenderly licking my lips causing my heart to
Wildly pant and my curly eyebrows to roll backwards
But I have to banish the stalwarts and move onwards

VAST DEPOSITORIES

You're like a sulken old poet
Quibbling over words n' verses
Fuelled with wine filled blood
Guilted in dark moonlit shades
Pertaining to the glimmer mottled night
Hearing the pleas of felling forest trees
By heartless and somewhat violent axe echoes
Scooping the viscosity of inglorious victories

Passing over wobbling frail, innocent territories
Lessened by inhumane disasters n' ruthless masters
How merciless is defeat whilst begging at your ruler's feet
Adrenalin declines steadily, as the fear surmounts credibly

There's an abundance of seemingly vast depositories
Idoling in the midst of unchattered, seas and skies
Can we believe there telling us nothing less than lies
How can we try to plunder, as much as is for you and I

VENOMOUS COMPLICATIONS

There are huge restoration procedures which
Have to strenuously put into commonplace
The allergic swelling reactions and severe life
Threatening venomous complications lye dismally

Hidden in damp darkened enclosures which
Are just as welcoming as uninvited guests
It's freakingly unimaginable to step out from the
Carbon monoxide var, onto a hydrogen sulphide mat

Without firstly resuscitating the pantyhose cat
There has to be an emergency antiseptic panacea
To infiltrate the fearsomely painful dizzy spasms
Circulating within the cuts n' bacterial abrasions

Penetrating in your puffed up bleeding wounds
Which are accumulating toxins; thus poisoning
Conveniently your antivenene cluster cul de sac
I'm not a preliminary herpetologist or a bionic

Genetic biologist or a desirable toxicologist
The curc is akin to a life caring hebologist
Who is crevice leaping whilst your softly sleeping
Can you carefully avoid the pent up costly weeping

VERY SWEET IS YOUR WAY

That was the last picture I had of you
It looked so faint n' pathetically blue
This saucy emotion. I lustfully refrain
For it pivotes like a hot burning flame

Standing on a stall so proud yet small
How bright you gleam as a guiding beam
Working you're way thru each n' everyday
Is very sweet; that's all I have to say

WISTFULLY MOPING

I'm wistfully moping at the delicately
Moondrenched skies unreliably spraying
Their contingent of asteroids n' comets n
Space junk vomits, a component of cosmic

Mystery is compelling our skeptical minds
There's a margin of transfer n' withdrawal
And of insufficient consultative measures
Stabbing at my poorly comprehending brain

Is our primitive knowledge scattered in vain?
Do we lack the disbursement of disclosing any
Permanent gain? Can we facilitate an enviable
Advantage, regardless from the cost and pain?

WHIPLASHING TAUNT

The lush symphony of life is bottle brushing
You're lavender scented hair, without a care
Fettering the malevolent whiplashing taunt
Suffusing the monotonous displeasing gaunt

Excitable persuassions keep wielding in our haunt
There's a certain agility shovel dusting futility
It's worth subscribing to this figurehead ability
The ladies eyes appraise onto the seersucker suit

The gentleman's composure is logistically mute
On the breadwinner's table there's fresh fruit
Our trawling lives are smuttily, scabbing deep
Once again we are orbiting in the nagging neap

WIN EVERY FIGHT

Get rid of that dolting cheerless look
And stop reading the super action book
There's no time for cornball comedies or
Lecherous wolf whistling calamities, our

Disgruntled opponents are prudish exponents
They don't favour pesty chatterbox twinings
I know your outspoken within a thumbtacked
World but we're heading for some tenebrous

High fallutin saga, in a realm which is miserably
Darker the chief courtesan is such a wild sparker
If you innately believe in justice and right; then
You must convincingly n' undeniably win every fight

WISHFULLY STARE

It's not the cyclonic, pounding acid rain that
Has scuttled your mascara down your podgy face
Your shimmering red lips are like sheer dynamite
And ambuing a flimsy hypnotic braggadocio effect

They're cold hearted; as you plainly select
Even though you frolic as the teacher's pet
Be careful not to get all wet. I'd like to throw
My hat high in the air because you lovingly care

Blindly I follow my heart, but your not there
Can I stop to see you or just wishfully stare
The winds of change are shifting us closer together
In a strange sort of labyrinth, we can live forever

ZEPHYR HUES

The suburban domestic life is very
Disarmingly innocuous, mixed within
A variable of intangible countenance
Inappropriate mediocrity and restless

Trite, that's why I'm now ready to bite
I can't bottle up my irrepressible agility
It's not confine to some in house ability
My barber indecorously adorns my roving

Hippy hirsute and smelly baggy pants
It appears like I've stumbled in from
The paltry chorus rain treading on silvery
Coloured zephyr hues, we can light the flues